THE NLP POCKETBOOK

By Gillian Burn
Drawings by Phil Hailstone

"Gillian has produced a 'gem' of a book – ensuring that a subject which, on face value, appears horrendously complex becomes easily understood and one that the reader can't wait to put into practice. I particularly enjoyed the cookie story!"
Gail Scott, Senior Manager, Occupational Health Services, HSBC

"Gillian Burn's NLP Pocket Book is beautiful in its simplicity and at the same time impressively comprehensive. Well organized and easy to read, the NLP Pocket Book takes the reader on a pragmatic and useful journey through the best of NLP. It is a wonderful overview and I highly recommend it for anyone interested in NLP."
Robert Dilts, NLP Author, Trainer and Co-developer

Published by:
Management Pocketbooks Ltd
Laurel House, Station Approach,
Alresford, Hants SO24 9JH, U.K.
Tel: +44 (0)1962 735573
Fax: +44 (0)1962 733637
E-mail: sales@pocketbook.co.uk
Website: www.pocketbook.co.uk

All rights reserved. No part of this publication may be reproduced, stored in a retrieval system or transmitted in any form, or by any means, electronic, mechanical, photocopying, recording or otherwise, without the prior permission of the publishers.

This edition published 2005.
Reprinted 2006.

© Gillian Burn 2005.

British Library Cataloguing-in-Publication Data – A catalogue record for this book is available from the British Library.

ISBN-13   978 1 903776 31 5
ISBN-10   1 903776 31 7

Design, typesetting and graphics by **efex ltd**.
Printed in U.K.

CONTENTS

INTRODUCTION 5
A brief introduction to NLP, what it is and who it is for, how it can help, setting intentions

THE FOUR KEY PRINCIPLES OF NLP 13
Building rapport, creating outcomes, developing your senses, flexibility

HOW NLP CAN MAKE A DIFFERENCE 31
Why it works, modelling, benefits in business, taking different perspectives on challenging situations

CONTENTS

BELIEVE IT OR NOT 39
The effect of beliefs, values, memories and past experiences, understanding how enabling and limiting beliefs may affect you, creating positive beliefs

LOOKING INSIDE THE BRAIN 49
Your brain, brain pathways, three regions, emotions and thinking, sleep, formation of habits, the habit virus, how you think, rewiring your thinking, conscious/unconscious mind, flashbulb memory, mind/body connection, a story about thinking

WHAT DID YOU SAY? 67
Language patterns, filters, your inner voice, negative and positive language, words to take care with, positive influence and persuasion

LOGICAL LEVELS OF CHANGE 85
Overview of different levels, how they can help, understanding and identifying them and using them

YOUR PERSONAL RESOURCES 95
Accessing your skills, nine rules, creating a resource bank, circle of excellence, creating anchors, future pacing and 'walking the SCORE' technique

COMPELLING ACTIONS 111
Belief assessment to identify barriers, the Time Line® process, realizing your goals, visualizing your success and making a start, GEO goal-setting model, creating mastery

'It is not the strongest of the species that survive, nor the most intelligent, but the most responsive to change.'
Charles Darwin

Introduction

INTRODUCTION
PERSONAL EXPERIENCE OF NLP

I was first introduced to NLP in 1999. I had just set up my own health consultancy, creating and delivering training courses and materials for corporate clients. I had heard about NLP and wanted to 'add some NLP' to my materials, or so I thought!

That was the start of a fascinating journey which continues to this day. By coincidence, or serendipity, I then spoke to a colleague who left a thought in my mind. Within days I had discovered a course about to start, created space in my diary and commenced my practitioner training. I followed this with Masters training, NLP health certification, and more. Each programme has provided invaluable information, skills, practical experience and confidence. I am indebted to the support from many, many people, and apologise for any omissions I may have made (see resources section). References are included throughout the book.

I continue to use NLP skills every day in my professional and personal life, in delivering training courses, in my writing, communication and coaching. I also unconsciously incorporate NLP principles in everything I do. As you use this book, I hope you will be able to explore some of the fascination and intrigue, and enjoy developing your own NLP skills in your personal and professional life.

INTRODUCTION

ACHIEVE EXCELLENCE WITH NLP

Every day you will interact with people by what you say, by what you do and by your body language, even if this is only in a facial reaction or a smile. The contact may be face-to-face, on the telephone or via e-mail. The interaction influences how you feel, how you may react to a certain situation and the effect you may have on others. Neuro-Linguistic Programming (NLP) provides the tools and techniques to help you at home and in the workplace to:

- Communicate effectively
- Motivate yourself and others
- Think positively
- Create actions to make a difference

The tools will help you understand how you and other people work, and provide you with skills to help achieve excellence in your personal and professional life.

INTRODUCTION

WHAT IS NLP?

NLP is described as the study of human excellence and demonstrates how to communicate effectively and influence others. It was developed in the 1970s by a group of psychologists who were studying successful people in order to analyse human behaviour. The group included Richard Bandler (psychologist), John Grinder (linguist) and Gregory Bateson (anthropologist). They considered styles of language, brain patterns and how words and actions are linked together to form certain programmes or sequences of behaviour.

Since then NLP has been developed further, providing a much greater understanding of thought processes, language patterns and human behaviour. It offers a process to help interpret human experiences, and to understand how people think, feel and react.

NLP is seen as a vital skill to improve the effectiveness and impact of communication. It aids understanding of human experiences and the relationship between the mind, body, emotions and actions. Using the language of the mind can help you achieve desired outcomes consistently.

'The psychology of excellence.'

'The difference that makes the difference in communication.'

INTRODUCTION

WHAT IS NLP?

Neuro – relates to the brain and what happens in your mind
Linguistic – relates to language and how you may use it
Programming – relates to patterns of behaviour which you learn and repeat

NEURO

The use of your senses to interpret the world around you. Neurological processes affect your thoughts and emotions, your physiology, and subsequent behaviour.

LINGUISTIC

How you use language to communicate with others and influence your experience.

PROGRAMMING

Internal thoughts and patterns of behaviour that help you evaluate situations, solve problems and make decisions.

INTRODUCTION

WHO IS NLP FOR?

NLP can be used throughout business, whether you work for a small organisation or a multinational. The skills are useful in communication, managing teams, project management, dealing with challenging situations and on any occasion when your work involves interacting with people. NLP can be used throughout business and education, during all stages of life.

The tools will help you gain an in-depth understanding of behaviour patterns and how individuals may respond in a variety of situations, and they will help you work more efficiently and effectively. Everyone can benefit from the skills, including, for example, business people, sports enthusiasts, actors, students, leaders, politicians and trainers.

Consider the following proverb, which aptly describes some of the key principles:

'If for a tranquil mind you seek, these things observe with care, of whom you speak, to whom you speak, and how, and when and where.'
Anon.

INTRODUCTION

HOW NLP CAN HELP

Think of some daily activities you are involved in:

- Meetings
- Communicating with team members
- Dealing with customers
- Sales or marketing of products
- Appraisals and interviewing
- Production planning
- Learning new information
- Studying, exams
- Preparing and delivering presentations

Add your own daily activities related to your work and have these in your mind as you read through the tools and techniques within this book. Consider how you can deal with situations in a different way in the future.

INTRODUCTION

SETTING YOUR INTENTION

Let's start by using NLP on you.

One of the principles of NLP is understanding what you want – your goals or outcomes. Just as you would tell a taxi driver where you want to go, having clear intentions helps you create the outcome you want. Consider your daily priorities from the previous page and set your personal intentions by answering the following questions:

- What do you want to improve?
- Which aspects of your work would you like to understand better?
- Why do you react in certain ways to different situations?
- Which habits or patterns of behaviour do you often repeat?
- Could you improve how you communicate with others?

Have these thoughts in your mind as you explore the key principles of NLP.

THE FOUR KEY PRINCIPLES OF NLP

THE FOUR KEY PRINCIPLES OF NLP

OVERVIEW OF PRINCIPLES

Underpinning NLP are four key principles. Understanding these principles at the outset will provide you with the foundations to build on as you explore the different NLP techniques.

Each of the principles relates to your own life and your life with other people. They focus on how you communicate, planning your goals and what you want to achieve in life, the skills you can use, and how to understand and respect differences in other people.

Whatever your profession or area of work, you will be able to consider which area of NLP interests you, which areas you feel at ease with and where you want to focus more time.

The key principles are:

THE FOUR KEY PRINCIPLES OF NLP

OVERVIEW OF PRINCIPLES

1. **Rapport**
   - Rapport with yourself – feeling at ease with your actions and your life journey
   - Building rapport in conversations and in interactions with others
   - Body language and the speed or pace of communication
   - Creating an understanding of situations from the other person's perspective

2. **Outcomes**
   - Focusing on the outcomes you want
   - Your intention, your goals in business and your personal life

3. **Senses**
   - Actively using all your senses: vision and sight, hearing and sound, feelings and touch, smell and aroma, and taste

4. **Flexibility**
   - Being flexible in your approach to situations, to create new perspectives
   - Understanding why you may interpret situations in a different way from other people

THE FOUR KEY PRINCIPLES OF NLP

1. RAPPORT

Rapport is essential for effective communication. It calls for mutual respect between people and is often achieved intuitively. It demands focus and concentration, so that you are present in the situation rather than wishing you were somewhere else!

Rapport involves showing a genuine interest, observing how a person reacts to what you say and identifying key words or phrases used. Rapport not only occurs in what you say, but also in your actions and body language which usually happen subconsciously.

How you communicate will depend on different situations and the method of communication, eg phone, e-mail, face-to-face.

To build rapport you need to be aware of how people communicate and how to use gestures, body position, tone of voice, words, etc.

THE FOUR KEY PRINCIPLES OF NLP

1. RAPPORT

MATCHING AND MIRRORING

One aspect of building rapport is the matching and mirroring technique, created by Milton Erickson in the early 1970s in his work with clinical hypnotherapy. It is linked to body language, where you endeavour to match the body language of the person to whom you are speaking. This can be seen clearly with new couples who, often subconsciously, copy the body positions of their partner – touching their hair in a similar way, both sitting or both standing, or leaning in the same way, etc. If you observe people in a restaurant or bar you can see how people may match and mirror other people in their group.

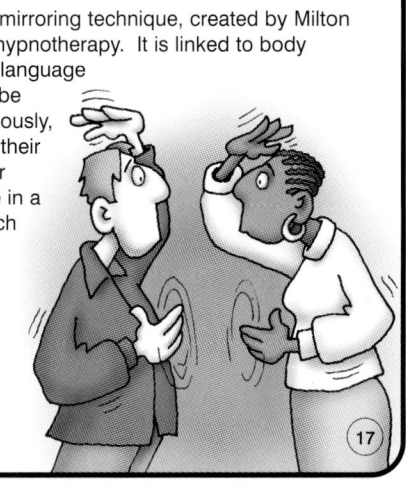

In normal communication, matching and mirroring usually occurs subtly and unconsciously. It involves being in a similar body posture to the other person and using similar gestures, styles of behaviour, and tone and speed of voice. It is an effective way to develop rapport with someone.

THE FOUR KEY PRINCIPLES OF NLP

1. RAPPORT

MATCHING AND MIRRORING – EXERCISE

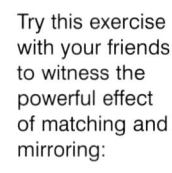

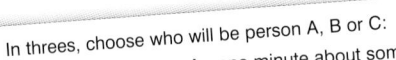

Try this exercise with your friends to witness the powerful effect of matching and mirroring:

In threes, choose who will be person A, B or C:

- Person A speaks for one minute about something they have really enjoyed, eg a holiday, party, hobby
- Person B listens and initially matches person A in body gestures and positions; then, person B does the opposite (ie mis-matches body language) while person A tries to keep speaking. Person B then reverts back to copying person A's body language, movements and position
- Person C observes the situation

The exercise involves matching body language, mis-matching and then matching again. After the exercise, swap roles so that each person tries each role. Allow person C to explain what they noticed while acting as the observer. Person A often finds it very difficult to keep speaking while person B is mis-matching body language.

Next time you are in a pub or restaurant, look around the room to see who is matching their companion's body language!

THE FOUR KEY PRINCIPLES OF NLP

1. RAPPORT

PACING AND LEADING

This technique is frequently useful, for example when you are coaching or if you are with someone who is distressed. You use pacing to match the pace of the other person's speech, only discussing the next topic when he or she is ready to move on. It is often described as PACE, PACE, PACE and then LEAD the conversation.

Imagine that something has upset you. Before you're able to think rationally about it, you often need to 'get it off your chest' by talking it through with a friend or colleague. Pacing works in a similar way. You need to allow someone to say what is important to them *first*, before you start discussing *your* agenda.

Example

When speaking to an elderly person, pace their speed of conversation before discussing your agenda. This may mean allowing them to discuss something that you consider irrelevant, but which is very important to them. Then they can pay attention and listen to what you need to say. If you interrupt people to encourage them to speak faster, you often achieve exactly the opposite effect!

THE FOUR KEY PRINCIPLES OF NLP

2. OUTCOMES

What do you want?

In the introduction you were asked to consider your outcome and intention.
It is important to have a clear outcome in your mind for any situation. This allows your unconscious mind to start processing information, almost as if you have antennae alert to any information that will be useful to you.

A clear outcome ensures you can focus your thoughts and subsequent communication appropriately, and effectively. It also helps you make the decisions and choices that are right for you.

Setting your outcome involves taking time to consider your goal or what you want to achieve – what will be important to you, what you will gain, and how it links into your overall plan professionally and personally.

Many people set goals and wonder why they have not achieved them. Often it is because they have focused on what they cannot do rather than on the positive steps needed to achieve their aim.

THE FOUR KEY PRINCIPLES OF NLP

2. OUTCOMES
SMART GOAL-SETTING

SMART goal-setting strategy helps provide a clearer focus in an agreed time frame.

SMART goal-setting is **S**pecific, **M**easurable, **A**chievable, **R**ealistic and within a defined **T**ime frame.

- **S** Specific and positive
- **M** Measurable and meaningful to you
- **A** Achievable and covering all areas of your life, stated in the present tense as if you have achieved it now
- **R** Realistic and right for you
- **T** Timed and targeted, towards what you want

In addition to SMART goal-setting, NLP incorporates a process called 'creating a well-formed outcome'.

THE FOUR KEY PRINCIPLES OF NLP

2. OUTCOMES

CREATING A WELL-FORMED OUTCOME

Creating a well-formed outcome involves asking a series of questions that will help you clarify your goal. They will help you to ascertain how important the goal is to you, how (if necessary) to revise it and how to make it more achievable.

Well-formed outcome questions:

1. Is the goal stated positively? What do you want? (Eg, wanting to **increase** company profits rather than a statement about **reducing** the loss.)

2. Can you start and maintain the process of achieving the goal by yourself, and keep it in your control?

3. Does the goal include all the senses? How will you know you have achieved it? What will you feel, see and hear when you have achieved it? What will other people feel, see and say when you have achieved it?

THE FOUR KEY PRINCIPLES OF NLP

2. OUTCOMES

CREATING A WELL-FORMED OUTCOME

4. Is the context clearly defined? How long will it take? Who will be involved? Where will it take place? How will it be achieved? When do you want it?
5. Have you checked that it is ecological or meaningful for you, ie is it worth the investment in time and money? Does the outcome fit in with your life and who you are?
6. Does the goal keep those aspects of the present situation you want to preserve, ie are there positive elements you wish to maintain?
7. Does it identify the resources you need – those you already have or those you need to acquire?
8. What first step must you take? What are the next steps?

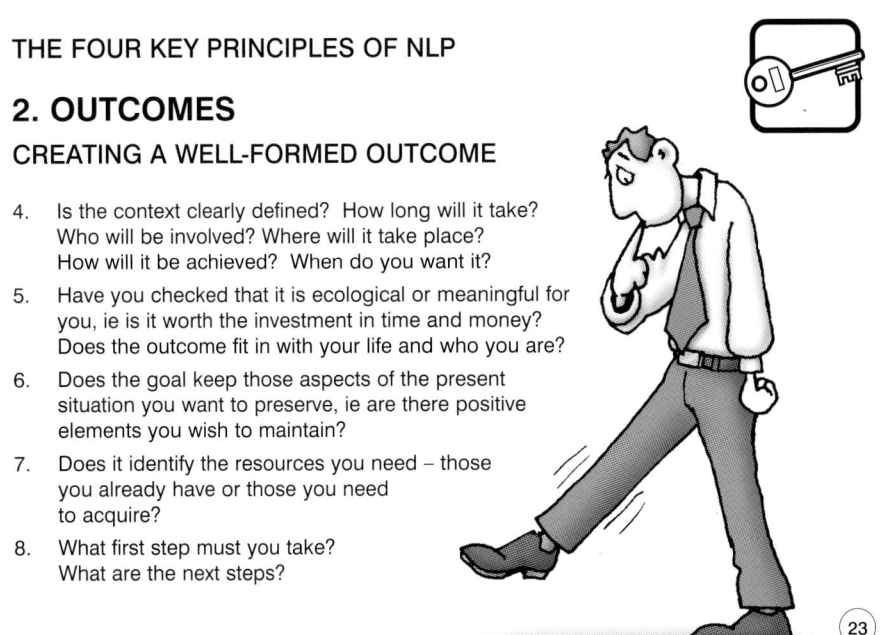

THE FOUR KEY PRINCIPLES OF NLP

3. SENSES

There are five main senses (seeing, hearing, feeling, taste and smell). You use these to make sense of the world around you. Using all the senses regularly can make communication more effective. They help you assess situations, analyse events and interpret your surroundings.

While everyone shares the same five senses, information is interpreted individually, eg some people love the smell of coffee, others cannot stand it! It helps to know how people interpret information and what their preferred sense is.

Consider a garden. One person may love the smell of freshly mown grass, another revels in the colours of the plants, while a third enjoys listening to birdsong. A scene can mean different things to different people depending on their preference for each sense. We register senses outside the body but the processing takes place inside, creating individual interpretations of events.

THE FOUR KEY PRINCIPLES OF NLP

3. SENSES

- **Visual** – what you see, pictures, use of colour and decoration, a preference for information presented graphically and pictorially
- **Auditory** – what you hear, sounds, voices, music, being able to process information presented verbally
- **Kinaesthetic** – what you feel, a preference for touch and to experience things personally, learn well by trying and doing
- **Olfactory** – what you smell (aroma), linked strongly to mood and memories

  NB: The sense of smell goes directly to the limbic system in the brain faster than the other senses. Women are thought to be 1000 times more sensitive to aromas than men!

- **Gustatory** – what you taste, responses linked to food and drink

In everyday communication, the first three senses are used most frequently. Think of a VHF radio to remember these three – **V**isual, **H**earing, and **F**eeling.

THE FOUR KEY PRINCIPLES OF NLP

3. SENSES

When the words/phrases below are used they give an indication of the speaker's dominant sense. Speaking to someone using the language of their preferred sense will increase rapport and enhance communication.

Consider which of the following words you use most frequently in order to ascertain your preferred sense:

VISUAL – SEEING

'I see what you mean'
'I get the picture'
'That looks right'
'I can imagine that'
'In my mind's eye'
'Show me the evidence'
'Let's take a long-term view'
'Keep an eye on things for me'

AUDITORY – HEARING

'I hear what you are saying'
'That sounds right'
'That rings a bell'
'Listen in to ...'
'That sounds familiar'
'Tune in to new ideas'
'I need to sound people out'
'He was on a different wavelength'

KINAESTHETIC – FEELING

'That feels right'
'I found it easy to handle'
'That touches a nerve'
'I can empathise with...'
'I've got the hang of that now'
'Hold on tight to reality'
'Keep a balance in your life'
'Get to grips with new trends'

THE FOUR KEY PRINCIPLES OF NLP

3. SENSES
SUBMODALITIES

Each sense can be refined with more detail. These finer distinctions are called submodalities. You can fine-tune the submodalities by adjusting the detail to change your feelings/emotions when dealing with positive and negative situations. Eg, by changing an image in your mind from colour to black and white you make it less vivid, and can then step back from the situation, disassociating yourself from the emotion. Or, you can bring humour into a challenging situation by imagining the other person as a cartoon character. Changes can be made at the time or afterwards when you allow your mind to think back.

VISUAL SUBMODALITIES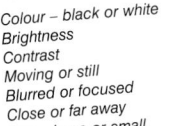

Colour – black or white
Brightness
Contrast
Moving or still
Blurred or focused
Close or far away
Size – large or small
In a frame or a panoramic view

AUDITORY SUBMODALITIES

Volume – loud or soft
Tone
Duration
Location
Stereo, mono or quadraphonic
Words or sounds
Pitch – high or low
Tempo and rhythm – fast or slow

KINAESTHETIC SUBMODALITIES

Temperature – hot or cold
Location
Intensity
Texture – rough or smooth
Weight – heavy or light
Pressure – hard or soft
Duration
Size

THE FOUR KEY PRINCIPLES OF NLP

4. FLEXIBILITY

Flexibility is about acknowledging that everyone interprets situations through their own perceptions, **thereby creating their own reality**.

Experiences are individual and each person will have their own unique interpretation of events. This will depend on how they experience the senses (sight, hearing, taste, feeling and smell) and how they interpret the information internally. Each person may create a different **'map of the world'**.

Situations also change with an ever-changing environment. Flexibility involves being open to change and working with the dynamics of change, rather than against it.

Example

Think of a balloon and describe it to me: what colour is it, what size and shape is it, where is it? If I ask several people there will be many different types and colours of balloons described since everyone will have different memories and ideas in their minds and, therefore, different perceptions of what a balloon looks like.

THE FOUR KEY PRINCIPLES OF NLP

4. FLEXIBILITY

Flexibility is also about having many choices, alternatives and options – especially if you don't achieve what you want the first time you try!

Being flexible allows you to gather information from a variety of sources, from different perspectives and from different points of view. As you gather more information you will be able to make more informed choices.

When you are surprised or annoyed by the other person's action, inaction or comments, remind yourself that they may perceive the situation from a different 'map of the world'. Understanding that we may all approach situations from a different perspective can alleviate anxiety and help us to be more tolerant of challenging and changing situations.

THE FOUR KEY PRINCIPLES OF NLP

4. FLEXIBILITY

EXAMPLE

Consider the following example, highlighting the different approaches to attending a meeting.

> **Example**
>
> Three business partners arranged to meet:
>
> **Danielle** arrived with a huge box file containing all their project materials, with the papers piled on top of each other in the box.
>
> **Sanjay** followed with labelled files, each organised to show previous meeting notes, project details, the financial report and the meeting agenda printed out for each person.
>
> **Peter** then dashed into the room late, without any papers, and asked Danielle if she had a pen and paper he could use!

Each person had a very different approach to preparing for the meeting and different styles of behaviour. This is the unique nature of individuals, and is part of the variety and flexibility required in business and personal life. Understanding these differences and how you may react lies at the heart of NLP.

How NLP can make a difference

HOW NLP CAN MAKE A DIFFERENCE

WHY IT WORKS

NLP helps you to unravel and interpret situations and to clarify your feelings and thoughts. It provides building blocks to move forward proactively and positively.

Initially, we need to understand how patterns of thoughts and behaviour are created and how we develop habits and mental programmes over time. We can then consider ways to re-programme our minds and create new neurological pathways to achieve success.

You store information in your mind based on your experiences and senses. The information is associated with certain people, places or situations and may be positive or negative. Understanding how to use the positive experiences to develop a resource bank is important, as is dealing with the negative situations in order to stop repeating old habits.

HOW NLP CAN MAKE A DIFFERENCE

MODELLING

One NLP technique is modelling what works well by identifying, and then copying, the best way to approach a situation. Modelling excellence involves finding out *how* someone does something well and replicating that excellence.

Examples

- As children grow up (especially between the ages of 7 and 14) certain aspects of their behaviour may be modelled on what they see in adults around them. Parents may wish to take note of this!
- In sport, people may model what a very good golfer or tennis player does, in order to improve their own game
- In business, the way employees behave is a reflection of the management style, eg the managing director walking around, being approachable, listening and responding or, conversely, creating a culture of dominance and submission

HOW NLP CAN MAKE A DIFFERENCE

BENEFITS IN BUSINESS

In business the challenges are numerous and varied. Consider some of the following challenges and how you can incorporate NLP:

- Communicating, eg learning to create rapport with others, understanding the use of all of the senses
- Goal-setting and achievement, eg visualizing success, modelling excellence, managing time
- Dealing with change, eg flexibility, being aware of different perspectives

Incorporating the principles of NLP into your business (and personal) life can help you discover new insights and different approaches, thus improving the way you interact and communicate with other people, and increasing your self-esteem and motivation.

HOW NLP CAN MAKE A DIFFERENCE

STANDING IN OTHER PEOPLE'S SHOES

This technique helps to provide a different perspective on challenging situations, business and personal. It involves being able to experience the situation or event in a different way, literally as if you were standing in someone else's shoes. In NLP this is called the **meta mirror**. Imagine looking out through each window in a house in turn, each time seeing a different aspect of the view of the garden.

In a challenging situation you may get 'stuck in a rut' by thinking about it in a certain way. The meta mirror technique helps you experience different perspectives, and consider alternative ways forward:

1. From your perspective – known as **first position**, ie in your shoes.
   What you want, feel and believe, irrespective of those around you.

2. Trying someone else's shoes – known as **second position**.
   Imagine the situation as the other person is experiencing it, from their perspective, or as they feel or see it.

3. The 'fly on the wall' approach – known as **third position**, ie an independent position as an observer to the situation. This allows the situation to be observed impartially from both sides.

HOW NLP CAN MAKE A DIFFERENCE

STANDING IN OTHER PEOPLE'S SHOES

The technique can be used for ordinary situations where a different perspective would be useful. It can also be applied to situations that are tense, angry, frightening, etc.

> **Example**
>
> Two colleagues, James and John, share an office. James is very organised and tidy; John is creative but disorganised and untidy.
>
> Imagine how James feels when he walks into the office to find all John's papers strewn over the floor and overflowing onto both desks. John leaves the office and when he returns he finds that James has tidied all the papers into neat piles, but John can't find anything!
>
> 1st position – James   2nd position – John   3rd position – 'fly on the wall'

HOW NLP CAN MAKE A DIFFERENCE

STANDING IN OTHER PEOPLE'S SHOES

ITEM 1
ITEM 2 ✓
ITEM 3
ITEM 4
ITEM 5

Imagining the situation as the other person sees it can be useful both at work and at home.

Considering an issue from all three perspectives often helps to alleviate a challenging situation, such as when something has been said or done that causes concern.

HOW NLP CAN MAKE A DIFFERENCE

THE NLP META MIRROR

Try the following exercise (originally developed by Robert Dilts in 1988) to provide different perspectives via the three perceptual positions. It helps to position three chairs in a room and physically move between each one as you do this.

First position: sit in the first chair to experience the situation from a personal perspective – what am I thinking, feeling, hearing, saying to myself and experiencing as I look across to the second chair, which represents the other person involved?

Second position: move to the second chair to imagine being the other person – what is he/she feeling, thinking and experiencing as he/she looks across to the 'person' in the first chair?

Third position: move to the third chair to observe both 'people' in the other chairs. Now consider how the two people respond to each other and to the situation. Observe yourself in first position and ask yourself what advice is needed.

You can repeat the exercise by re-visiting the chairs to see how you feel and how the situation may have changed with a different perspective. Be aware of any change in your interpretation of the event and how alternative options may now be apparent. You may feel differently about the person or situation now.

BELIEVE IT OR NOT

BELIEVE IT OR NOT

PRESUPPOSITIONS

Underpinning NLP is a series of presuppositions or beliefs which are developed during your life, based on practical experiences. They are called presuppositions as individuals presuppose them to be true.

While you may be consciously aware of some presuppositions, there will be others that you do not know about until they are pointed out to you. When you are consciously aware of them, you can decide if you believe they are true or not, and how they may help you with a particular situation. Examples of presuppositions include:

'The map is not the territory – my mental map of the world is different from yours'
This is one of the fundamental presuppositions in NLP and implies that your experience is always slightly separated from reality. Practising NLP involves changing the maps, not reality. It reflects how you experience the world though your own senses, creating your own personal map in your head. The internal map is never an exact copy of the real situation. Your map will also be different from someone else's map.

BELIEVE IT OR NOT

PRESUPPOSITIONS

'You have within yourself all the resources you need to achieve what you want'
To be able to use the resources, you need to know that you have the resources and how to use them. You may also need to acquire new resources as you learn and grow. The emphasis is on your internal thoughts and creating a resourceful state of mind.

'Every behaviour has a positive intention'
Every behaviour aims to achieve something valuable and happens for a reason. This can relate to your behaviour and that of others. However, you may interpret the behaviour as negative, even though it was positively intentioned.

'There is no failure, only feedback'
The brain works by trial and error – even if someone has not succeeded yet, they still have the opportunity to do so. During your life you may make many mistakes. However, you can choose how you react and how you learn from each mistake. Mistakes can become opportunities for learning and growth.

BELIEVE IT OR NOT

PRESUPPOSITIONS

'The meaning of communication is the response it elicits'
People respond to what they think you mean, which can be an accurate or inaccurate interpretation of your intended meaning. In this context, communication includes both verbal and non-verbal signs. This presupposition highlights the importance of talking to people instead of at them and being aware of how people respond to what you say (ie what they have heard) and adjusting your communication accordingly.

'The mind and body are interconnected; if you affect one, you affect the other'
Modern science has clearly shown the link between the mind and the body. The immune system is integrally linked to brain activity, eg mental stress can inhibit the performance of the immune system, reducing your ability to combat illness. Thoughts are transported throughout your body via neurotransmitters. These chemicals transmit messages along nerves and between cells, creating a form of communication between the brain and the rest of your body, so in effect your body is expressing your thinking.

BELIEVE IT OR NOT

BELIEFS, MEMORIES AND VALUES

Your beliefs, memories, values and experiences affect how you perceive, and interpret, current life events and business challenges. They can have emotions attached to them, affecting how you deal with current situations.

Beliefs include things you trust as being true and what you believe you can or cannot do. Beliefs can be positive, creating success, or be negative and limit your behaviour. You form beliefs in many unconscious ways, influenced by parents, teachers, friends, etc. You can also be affected by other people's negative beliefs or preconceptions of what they think you can or cannot do. For example, think about the effect of a supportive, positive manager genuinely praising an employee or, conversely, a manager who continually complains about an employee.

Beliefs help you make sense of the world around you and can either empower you to achieve success or limit your thinking about progress.

BELIEVE IT OR NOT

BELIEFS, MEMORIES AND VALUES

Memories can affect your present and future. Previous memories can form the basis of your reaction to present situations. New experiences can bring back old memories and emotions, so that you react to the old memory and emotion rather than experiencing the current situation. This can lead unconsciously to a negative response. For example, having failed exams at school you may now not feel confident sitting professional exams.

Values are like an evaluation filter, interpreting what is important to you and what makes you feel good. You create values from all around you, eg family, friends, school, media or colleagues. Values drive your behaviour and can either motivate or demotivate you. Values also affect your choice of friends, hobbies, interests and how you spend your time. Examples of values include honesty, caring, success, financial security, support and openness.

BELIEVE IT OR NOT

WHY BELIEFS ARE IMPORTANT

Your experiences are coded, ordered, stored and replayed through language and other forms of communication (pictures, sounds, feelings, tastes, smells). They are stored in your mind until similar situations or events occur.

If you have stored the experience in a negative way, as soon as a similar situation arises, your mind recalls the previous unhappy experience. This affects your beliefs and fuels a negative reaction in your body.

The nature of beliefs and memories is that much of what you remember is fabricated by your mind in order to fit in with what you think *must* have happened. You will remember what you want of a certain situation.

BELIEVE IT OR NOT

BELIEFS OF EXCELLENCE

You can change a negative belief or value by changing the way you think about an experience. One way is to consider how you use your senses when thinking about certain beliefs and values. You can adjust the submodalities – eg the colour of the picture, intensity of the feeling or sound of the memory – to diminish the sensation so that you adjust how you think about it. You can then increase the positive beliefs or values you would like to try out.

To achieve excellence or success, try out a belief as if it were true. If it works for you, then that positive belief is more likely to stay with you and help you achieve further excellence. You are removing any limitations you may have accumulated through memories or previous experience.

Consider Roger Bannister who broke the record for running the mile. At the time, people believed it was physically impossible for a man to run a mile in under four minutes. It took Roger nine years' preparation and many attempts before he eventually beat the time in May 1954. The 4-minute barrier was then broken again only six weeks later, and over the next nine years more than 200 people broke the record. The belief that it was impossible had been changed.

BELIEVE IT OR NOT

ENABLING AND LIMITING BELIEFS

Our beliefs can be positive and enabling – or limiting and negative.

Enabling beliefs with a positive impact ➕

'I can do that'
'I'm good at…'
'I achieve my goals'
'I'm learning a new skill'
'Being different is good'
'I can do that if you help me'
'I can see the glass is half full with space for more'
'Let me have a go'

Limiting beliefs with a negative impact ➖

'Failing an exam is painful'
'I can't sing'
'I'm useless at…'
'I was never any good at…'
'I always do it wrong'
'I can't do …as well as…'
'I'm too…short, thin, fat, tall'
'It is too difficult'
'They won't like me'

Consider which of the above examples you identify with, to see whether you are more inclined to use limiting or enabling beliefs.

BELIEVE IT OR NOT

CREATING A POSITIVE BELIEF
EXERCISE

Think of a situation that is worrying you, that is due to happen some time in the future, eg a potentially difficult business meeting, challenging conversation, or important presentation.

1. In your mind's eye imagine the event occurring in the future. You may find you look up and in front of you as you consider the event.
2. Now look further out into the future, as if you were floating out in time to 15 minutes after the successful completion of the event. Be aware of what you see, hear and feel, and bring in all the senses that have recorded the event successfully happening.
3. Next, think again about the event itself and notice how you feel about the success, now in the present time.
4. Remaining in the present moment, consider how your level of concern or anxiety has altered.

This technique helps to change the limiting belief by allowing your mind to practise the event happening successfully, almost like a mental rehearsal. When the event actually occurs, it has already been practised, reducing your anxiety and giving you more confidence.

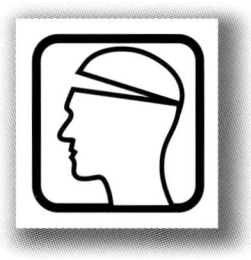

LOOKING INSIDE THE BRAIN

LOOKING INSIDE THE BRAIN

YOUR BRAIN

The 'Neuro' part of NLP addresses what is happening in your brain and how you think about experiences and interactions with others.

Understanding how you create thoughts, and how brain pathways develop, can provide insights to explain how you deal with certain situations, consciously and unconsciously.

Learning how to change habits and rewire your thinking can be a valuable tool to creating greater flexibility and new approaches to challenging situations.

Brain facts

- Weighs 1400gms – equivalent to 1$^1/_2$ bags of sugar
- Made up of 75-80% water, 10% fat, 8% protein
- Contains 10-15 billion neurons (brain cells) and, contrary to popular belief, the body generates 1000's of new brain cells every day

LOOKING INSIDE THE BRAIN

YOUR BRAIN

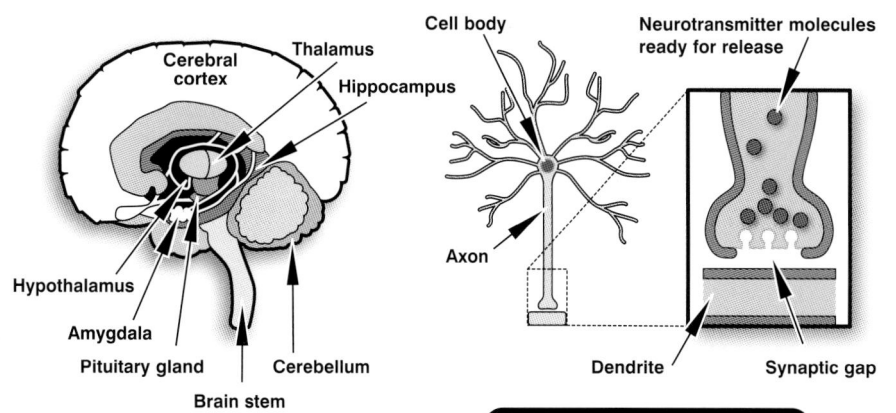

- Cerebral cortex
- Thalamus
- Hippocampus
- Hypothalamus
- Amygdala
- Pituitary gland
- Cerebellum
- Brain stem

- Cell body
- Axon
- Dendrite
- Synaptic gap
- Neurotransmitter molecules ready for release

A Neuron and Synapse

LOOKING INSIDE THE BRAIN

NEURONS AND BRAIN PATHWAYS

Brain cells or neurons are responsible for your thinking. As you think, imagine or learn something, messages are passed between brain cells forming a neural pathway. Each neuron communicates by releasing chemicals called neurotransmitters, which carry messages between the neurons.

Dendrites and **axons** connect each neuron. Dendrites receive information and axons transmit it. Between each neuron is a tiny gap or synapse, across which the neurotransmitters pass.

The brain is constantly changing as synaptic connections between neurons grow and become more established. If the connections are not used, they grow weak and eventually die away.

Regular use keeps them strong and healthy. Intellectual activity stimulates growth and enhances connections of neurons. The motto, 'use it or lose it' is worth remembering.

You have infinite potential in your brain, and may use less than 5% of the potential!

> *'The brain is the most complex organ in the body and one with the greatest capacity to re-invent itself.'*
> **Professor Robert Winston**

LOOKING INSIDE THE BRAIN

THINKING

The three regions of the brain involved in thinking are:

Cerebral cortex
- Left and right cerebrum, called the 'thinking cap'
- Processes visual, auditory and touch data, and controls intellectual processes – talking, seeing, hearing, reasoning, thinking
- This area considers a situation and decides how to react, based on previous memories

Mammalian brain (limbic system)
- Contains the amygdala, hypothalamus, thalamus, and hippocampus
- Plays a vital role in long-term memory
- Controls emotion, sexuality, health, and the immune system
- Maintains blood pressure, heart rate, temperature and blood sugar levels

Reptilian brain (brain stem)
- Controls breathing, heart rate, sleep
- Detects sensory information, controls temperature and digestion

LOOKING INSIDE THE BRAIN

LIMBIC SYSTEM IN EMOTIONS AND THINKING

The limbic system is known as the 'seat of our emotions'. As information travels into the limbic system, it is connected to an emotion or memory to store the data within the brain. The emotions are then filed away until needed.

Amygdala – an almond shaped structure where we feel emotions.
Hypothalamus – the processing centre, receiving information and sending out appropriate messages. Also controls the pituitary gland which releases hormones including those related to flight-or-fight responses.
Thalamus – responsible for the connection of sensory information.
Hippocampus – stores and retrieves long-term memories and reaches maturity around three years old.
Corpus callosum – connects left and right hemispheres of the brain to allow communication between each side (a key aspect in thinking and behaviour).

Why women may be different from men!
The corpus callosum is slightly larger in women, contains more neural connections and enables the brain to communicate more quickly between different regions. Research suggests that this aspect assists women in their ability to multi-task, communicate, express emotions and understand those of other people!

LOOKING INSIDE THE BRAIN

AND WHEN WE SLEEP...

Sleep provides an important time for memorising and learning. The brain is able to mull over information when we are asleep, reinforcing new patterns and etching them into our memory. We master tasks more quickly with adequate sleep.

Dreaming is when our unconscious mind processes the day's events, sorting through the memories, learning from experiences and planning for the future. Dreams can help our memory clear itself of what is not needed.

'During dreams, our neurotransmitters help to clear memories, preserve the relevant and junk the extraneous!'
James Bower, 1993

'Dreams are the brain's waste paper basket.'
Francis Crick and Graeme Mitchison, 1983

(See further: *The Human Mind and How to Make the Most of it* by Professor Robert Winston)

LOOKING INSIDE THE BRAIN

FORMATION OF HABITS

When you learn a new skill, a new pattern is established in the brain. Each time you repeat the skill, the pattern becomes clearer, strengthening the connection between brain cells. This process builds the new pattern or habit into the chemistry of the human brain. The more you practise a new skill, the more the connections grow in the brain.

> *'As you learn, the circuitry of your brain learns too.'*
> **Professor Robert Winston, 2003**

Imagine walking though a previously unexplored forest – if you are followed by 200 other people, the pathway becomes much clearer. In the same way, pathways and patterns of behaviour are developed in the brain.

When you learn to drive a car, it takes a little time to get used to the controls and procedures to drive safely. However, it soon becomes second nature as you develop the new brain pathways to know what to do. In a similar way, if you consider a journey you regularly make, there may be occasions when you feel you are driving on automatic pilot. You may even find one day that you take the journey unnecessarily, as your mind is programmed into the familiar route.

LOOKING INSIDE THE BRAIN

THE HABIT VIRUS

In a research study, five monkeys were placed in a cage with a ladder leading to a bunch of ripe bananas. One monkey headed towards the bananas, but hidden at the top of the ladder was a water spray which showered water over the monkey. So it abandoned the attempt. Another monkey tried; it too was sprayed with water. Each monkey in turn tried, but each was doused and eventually gave up.

The researchers turned off the water spray and removed one monkey from the cage, replacing it with a new one. The new monkey saw the bananas and immediately tried to climb the ladder. However, to its horror, the other monkeys leapt up and stopped it. Over time the researchers removed and replaced all the original monkeys. Every time a newcomer approached the ladder the other monkeys stopped it from climbing up. None of the remaining monkeys had ever been sprayed, but still no monkey approached the ladder to reach the bananas. As far as they knew that was the way it had always been done, and so the habit was formed.

Similarities with how company policy begins and other business practices?

LOOKING INSIDE THE BRAIN

HOW YOU THINK

The thoughts within your brain determine your reaction to situations and how you may communicate with someone or interpret a particular event.

Your thoughts affect your emotions and subsequent behaviour to others. By rewiring your thinking you can have a positive effect on your emotions and behaviour.

Rewiring your thinking is a valuable tool to help create new pathways and new habits. These examples highlight where rewiring may be helpful:

- Gaining a new perspective
- Trying something new
- Replacing negative thoughts with positive ones
- Exchanging limiting thoughts with enabling thoughts
- Encouraging new ideas and creativity
- Altering old habits
- Developing new approaches to situations

LOOKING INSIDE THE BRAIN

REWIRING YOUR THINKING

1
'I can't, it won't work'
The negative pathway is developed.

2
'I can't, it won't work'
The negative pathway becomes a habit.

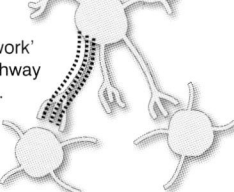

3
'I can, it may work'
A new pathway is created.

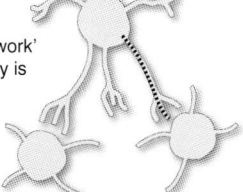

4
'I can, it will work'
The new positive habit is created.

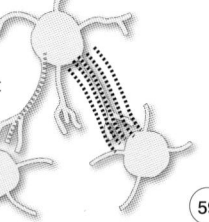

LOOKING INSIDE THE BRAIN

REWIRING YOUR THINKING

To rewire your thinking you need to be willing to take risks and occasionally do things differently. Even driving to or from work a different way encourages flexibility and encourages new brain pathways to develop.

> **Exercise**
> Fold your arms in front of your body and then re-cross them the other way. You may find the second way feels uncomfortable. The more you repeat this exercise the more familiar it will feel and the more the brain pathway develops and gets used to the new habit.

In the same way, we can develop new thoughts, new ways of thinking and different approaches to situations. With a new skill the new brain pathways will take time to develop. For example, if you are learning a new tennis stroke, it may take a great deal of practice until you start to master the new skill. The more you practise, the more you learn!

It is estimated that it takes 21 days to create a new habit and to allow the new brain pathways to develop to the point where the new process becomes familiar.

LOOKING INSIDE THE BRAIN

CONSCIOUS/UNCONSCIOUS MIND

BRAIN'S RESPONSE TO NEGATIVES

Your unconscious mind does not know the difference between what is real and what is imagined, and does not process negative words directly. The unconscious mind has difficulty understanding negatives.

The brain deletes negatives and works more efficiently with positive commands.
The brain ignores the word 'don't' in a sentence and only thinks about *'do'*.
If you say, *'Don't think of a blue elephant'*, your mind first has to think about one!

You need to say what you actually want someone to do; think about the words they will be hearing. Say it the way you want it!

Inappropriate use:	Alternative use:
'Don't shout'	'Stay calm'
'Don't do that'	'Try this instead'
'Don't miss your targets'	'Let me know when you reach the target'
'Don't worry'	'Take time to relax'
'Stop criticising'	'Point out the positive'
'It's a problem'	'I can do that for you'
'You can't miss it'	'It's easy to find'
'Don't take this route'	'Go this way'

LOOKING INSIDE THE BRAIN

WHAT OUR UNCONSCIOUS MIND RESPONDS TO

- **Chunk size 7 +/- 2 facts** – your mind can usually deal with seven plus or minus two bits of information at any one time, deleting the rest! *(American Psychologist, George Miller, Harvard, 1956).* Eg, if a telephone number is grouped in threes, it is often easier to remember: 591 624 958.
- The mind needs **repetition** of information and regular review to enhance memory and generate a **habit**. Eg: repeating key information at the end of a presentation or lecture, repeating a new task you are learning for the first time until it feels more familiar, reviewing new material the next day and at regular intervals afterwards
- The mind responds well to **symbols** as they increase the speed of interpretation and are very effective for people with a strong visual sense. In addition, visual cues encourage both sides of the brain to work together, further securing the message, eg:

Symbols link in with the visual memory and are faster for the mind to respond to at a glance.

LOOKING INSIDE THE BRAIN

'FLASHBULB' MEMORY

A phenomenon called 'flashbulb' memory occurs when you are able to recall and remember specific details related to a significant event. For example, you may remember exactly where you were and what you were doing when you heard about the events of Sept 11th 2001, or the death of Princess Diana or the assassination of President Kennedy.

To help your mind remember and recall information, your conscious mind needs to associate the information with emotion, events or novelty facts. The novelty of the incoming information and the intensity of the emotion, along with the frequency with which the information is repeated or encountered, will help determine how indelibly a memory is stored.

LOOKING INSIDE THE BRAIN

MIND/BODY CONNECTION

The connection between your mind and body is becoming much better understood. How you think and feel emotionally will affect your health and how you feel physically. Your unconscious mind will also influence your subsequent actions and behaviour.

New research in the area of psycho-neuro-immunology has been exploring how the mind-body connection may affect your immune system and health (Dr C.B. Pert, 1997). When you feel good in yourself, you have a better chance of remaining healthy. Conversely, when you are feeling unhappy or depressed, your immune system will be depleted.

- Fearful emotions can deplete the immune system and negatively affect your health
- Happiness and laughter help secrete endorphins ('happy hormones') which, in turn, help to improve health and recovery

LOOKING INSIDE THE BRAIN

HOW THOUGHTS AFFECT YOUR DESTINY

Watch your thoughts, they become words

Watch your words; they become actions

Watch your actions; they become habits

Watch your habits; they become character

Watch your character; it becomes your destiny.

Frank Outlaw

LOOKING INSIDE THE BRAIN

THE COOKIE THIEF STORY

A woman was waiting at an airport and bought a book and a bag of cookies. She sat down placing her bags beside her. As she read her book she noticed the man next to her starting to eat cookies from the bag between them. She tried to ignore this, not wanting to make a scene, but couldn't believe he could so blatantly steal her cookies.

She became increasingly irritated as every time she took a cookie he took one too. Finally, there was only one left in the bag. She wondered what he would do. He smiled and, laughing, took the last one and broke it in half. He then offered her half, while he ate the other. She snatched her half from him, astonished by his rudeness and lack of gratitude.

The woman sighed with relief when her flight was called and headed to the gate. Sinking in her seat, she reached in her bag for her book. However, gasping with surprise, she saw her bag of cookies right in front of her eyes! She realized that if her cookies were in her bag, then the others were his and he had been trying to share! It was now too late to apologise, as she realized with horror that she was in fact the rude one, and the true 'cookie thief'.

WHAT DID YOU SAY?

WHAT DID YOU SAY?

LANGUAGE PATTERNS

How you communicate through language is a key area of NLP. What you say and how you say it affects other people and can influence or persuade them in different ways. You need to listen very clearly to what is being said, to notice the style of phrases/words used by the other person.

Style of language often occurs unconsciously and communication can be enhanced when people use similar styles. Language patterns, known in NLP as **meta programmes**, develop throughout your life. Different life experiences will often change how you use these patterns.

Through the words used, language patterns indicate how people perceive and interpret situations. For example, some people just like to hear the 'big picture', whereas others prefer to know all the minute details – known as 'big chunk' and 'small chunk' styles.

WHAT DID YOU SAY?

LANGUAGE PATTERNS

META PROGRAMMES

Understanding your own preferences and other people's can help in building rapport and in communicating effectively. People with similar language patterns often show similar patterns of behaviour. For meta programmes to be effective you have to use words and phrases appropriate for the other person – saying the *right* thing, in the *right* way at the *right* time.

Pinpoint which meta programme the other person usually adopts and phrase your communication using the same one. This can help the person hear and understand what you are saying faster and more effectively.

Someone, for example, who uses a 'moving away from' meta programme will respond better to a request to get on with their work if you say, 'because you won't have to stay late' rather than, 'because you can go home early'.

Some examples of the numerous meta programmes follow.

WHAT DID YOU SAY?

LANGUAGE PATTERNS
EXAMPLES OF META PROGRAMMES

MOVING AWAY FROM

Style: avoid, exclude, recognise problems, not have, prevent
Away from the negative, avoiding problems

You need to: use words/phrases which take the person **away from** a situation, eg:

'If you don't do that project, you can work on…'
'If you don't meet the target…'

MOVING TOWARDS

Style: gain, attain, get, include, target, achieve, accomplish
Towards the positive, goal-oriented

You need to: use words/phrases which take the person **towards** a target, eg:

'Let's aim for 20% more calls next week.'
'The benefit of achieving a bonus...'

BIG CHUNK – GLOBAL

Style: overview, big picture, random order
Generalities

You need to: use words/phrases about the big picture, eg:

'What will this mean overall?'

SMALL CHUNK – DETAIL

Style: details, sequences, exactly, precise
Details and specifics

You need to: use words/phrases about minute details, eg:

'By the 3rd quarter of next year the growth will be 15%.'

WHAT DID YOU SAY?

LANGUAGE PATTERNS

EXAMPLES OF META PROGRAMMES

INTERNAL

Style: know within self, use own feelings
Locus of control is 'self', happy to make own decisions

You need to: use words/phrases about personal feelings, eg:

'You decide, it's up to you.'

EXTERNAL

Style: depend on others, facts and figures
Locus of control is on other person – needs feedback

You need to: use words/phrases about other people, eg:

'My boss says I can't do that.'
'Other people have found that this works.'

TIME ORIENTATION : PAST

Style: concentrate on past
Focus on the past

You need to: use words/phrases about the past, eg:

'Last time I gave this presentation…'

TIME ORIENTATION : FUTURE

Style: look to future
Focus on the future

You need to: use words/phrases about the future, eg:

'In five years' time, I want to be…'

WHAT DID YOU SAY?

LANGUAGE PATTERNS
EXAMPLES OF META PROGRAMMES

OPTIONS

Style: try new ways, offer choices
Love variety and different possibilities
Start projects but don't always finish them

You need to: use words/phrases about options, eg:

'You could order it in any colour you prefer.'

PROCEDURES

Style: follow set rules
Follow set methods, rules, procedures
Like precise instructions, follow speed limits!

You need to: use words/phrases with clear procedures, eg:

'You need to follow steps 1- 10 precisely.'

PRO-ACTIVE

Style: get things done, take control, take action
Like taking charge, find solutions
Move at a faster pace

You need to: use words/phrases about action, eg:

'You can do it this way, now.'

REACTIVE

Style: wait for others to take the lead
Analyse choices and goals, wait for instructions
Slower pace, think about things

You need to: use words/phrases with choices, eg:

'Let's wait to see what the manager says.'

WHAT DID YOU SAY?

LANGUAGE PATTERNS

META PROGRAMME PREFERENCES

Think of the phrases you are more likely to use from the previous examples and ✔ the box which represents your preferences:

Moving away from	☐	☐	☐	☐	☐	Moving towards
Big chunk	☐	☐	☐	☐	☐	Small chunk
Internal	☐	☐	☐	☐	☐	External
Time orientation: past	☐	☐	☐	☐	☐	Time orientation: future
Options	☐	☐	☐	☐	☐	Procedures
Pro-active	☐	☐	☐	☐	☐	Reactive

WHAT DID YOU SAY?

LANGUAGE FILTERS

In conversation we unconsciously use three filters or processes – deletion, distortion and generalization (described by Richard Bandler as the *'engine that drives NLP'*). The filters transform what we experience with our senses into our internal thoughts. They clarify our experiences and help us to interpret the true meaning behind what people say. They can work positively and negatively.

You can identify the filter a person is using by listening to signs in their language (see examples on pages 77-79). When you recognise the pattern being used you can ask specific questions to ascertain the true meaning of their communication. (The specific questions were originally developed by Richard Bandler and John Grinder in 1975, and are referred to in NLP as the 'Meta Model'.)

WHAT DID YOU SAY?

LANGUAGE FILTERS

The filters are:

Deletion – being selective about experiences and choosing to omit certain information, so part of the meaning is deleted, eg saying a project is going well because the milestones have been met, but omitting to say that the costs have escalated and the project is now over budget.

Distortion – creating, from other people's words or actions, a meaning which may not necessarily be true or which may be based on minimal evidence, eg someone in the office laughing and you believe they are laughing at you; or your partner buying you flowers and you believing this means they love you.

Generalization – believing something to be universally true based on limited experience. If you generalize incorrectly the overall meaning may be missed. With generalizations you unconsciously develop rules and beliefs which may be true or untrue. Words often used include: all, never, every, always. Eg: *'I know I always upset someone at team meetings'*.

WHAT DID YOU SAY?

LANGUAGE FILTERS
META MODEL QUESTIONS

With a language filter identified, questions can be phrased more specifically to gain greater understanding. Questioning helps to:

- Gather more information to find what may have been left out
- Clarify meaning, when evidence has been distorted from the true meaning
- Identify a limitation, to offer more choices when information has been generalized

WHAT DID YOU SAY?

LANGUAGE FILTERS
META MODEL QUESTIONS

FILTER	Deletion – omitting information	
Examples of language used		**Questions to ask**
'That was good.'		*'What aspect is good, specifically?'*
'He made me angry.'		*'In what way?'*
'Customers can make it very difficult.'		*'Which customer?' 'How will it be difficult?'*
AIM	To gather additional information to obtain a clear outcome or clarify the message.	
HOW	Ask questions to obtain more information, eg 'Tell me more, what other information do you have, where, when, how, what, who?' Use: 'exactly, specifically, precisely'.	

WHAT DID YOU SAY?

LANGUAGE FILTERS
META MODEL QUESTIONS

FILTER Distortion – changing the meaning

Examples of language used	Questions to ask
'Wearing that tie means you don't take this job seriously.'	*'What specifically about this tie makes you think that?'*
'Sitting at the company dinner next to the Managing Director means you will be promoted.'	*'How does this guarantee promotion?'*
'Your comment made me upset.'	*'How exactly did what I say make you feel upset?'*

AIM To ascertain the underlying meaning.

HOW Ask questions related to how you know and what the evidence is.
Use: 'Who says?' 'How do you know?'

WHAT DID YOU SAY?

LANGUAGE FILTERS
META MODEL QUESTIONS

FILTER Generalization – taking specific experiences and creating a general principle (eg, using words such as: all, never, every, always)

Examples of language used	Questions to ask
'Everything is going wrong.'	'Everything or just one aspect?'
'This always happens.'	'Always or just occasionally?'
'Everyone gets in the way.'	'Everyone or just someone?'

AIM	To expand the conversation away from the limits the person is setting.
HOW	Ask questions to ascertain if it happens every time and if it is always the case. Use: 'Every time?' 'What would happen next?' 'What stops you?'

Ref. Richard Bandler and John Grinder, 1975.

WHAT DID YOU SAY?

YOUR INNER VOICE

Your inner voice can be very powerful and rather loud! It links in with your unconscious mind and can provide important messages and answers to problems. Acknowledge what your inner voice is saying and then ask yourself:

- Is this a helpful thought?
- What would be a more positive thought?
- Does my inner voice have a warning/message I need to be aware of?
- Is there a positive reason/intention behind the message from my inner voice?

Every thought in your mind is passed via neurotransmitters around the body, linking mind and body together. How you feel physically and emotionally affects your performance. Being aware of your inner voice and thoughts can provide the answers to issues or challenges and help you respond more resourcefully and positively.

WHAT DID YOU SAY?

NEGATIVE AND POSITIVE LANGUAGE
(LINKED TO LIMITING AND ENABLING BELIEFS)

Negative thoughts, eg:
- Everything I do goes wrong
- No one likes me
- I will never get it right
- It just won't work

It is estimated that there are more than three times as many words in the English language to express negatives as there are for positives!

Practise exchanging your negative thoughts for positive ones, which are more rational and helpful, eg:
- What is going well in my life?
- Who am I getting on well with?
- Which aspects of the project have I already done?
- What is working?

WHAT DID YOU SAY?

WORDS TO TAKE CARE WITH!

The following words need to be used with caution:

- **BUT** – Negates anything before it. Instead use, *'And next time, let's do...'*

- **SHOULD** – Creates an instruction and, possibly, a sense of guilt.

- **DON'T** – Leads the brain to associate with the negative aspect first, before it hears the real message. Eg: *'Don't think about the project yet'*, encourages the listener to think about the project first, in order to stop thinking about it!

- **TRY** – Carries the expectation that you may fail to do something.

- **WHY?** – Implies that you need to justify something. Alternatively use *How?*

WHAT DID YOU SAY?

POSITIVE INFLUENCE AND PERSUASION

Language can be very powerful and can trigger emotional reactions. Paying attention to language can help to highlight patterns of behaviour. People who use similar patterns of language often achieve greater rapport more quickly than people who don't. To influence and persuade others positively:

- Listen carefully to what is being said and how it is said – this may highlight a preferred language style. As they say, 'You have two ears and one mouth...'

- Match the pace of the conversation, remembering the stages of *pace, pace, pace* and then *lead*

- Match language styles and meta programmes – use words/phrases similar to those favoured by the other person (eg, big picture or detail, moving towards a goal or away from a problem)

WHAT DID YOU SAY?

POSITIVE INFLUENCE AND PERSUASION

- Note the meta model the person is using – are they deleting or distorting information or generalizing?
- Consider your agenda and the other person's. Ascertain what's important to them before rushing in with all your questions – ie practise behavioural flexibility and be open to other ideas
- Create a situation of respect for each person
- Ask appropriate questions to drill down for the information you require – *'What is it you want, specifically?' 'What is stopping you moving forward?' 'How will you do this?'*
- Adopt positive language – no negative words that the unconscious mind will focus on
- Use all the senses to enrich your communication

Logical Levels of Change

LOGICAL LEVELS OF CHANGE

OVERVIEW

'Logical levels', an NLP term, identifies specific categories of information used during communication and which affect rapport. Developed by Robert Dilts based on a model of change originated by Gregory Bateson, it is also called 'neurological levels' – denoting that it relates to thoughts occurring in the mind.

The levels or categories relate to how you think about situations. Each level provides different information to help understand what may be going on or where you may be experiencing difficulty in moving forward.

There are five main levels with an optional sixth depending on the context. They are like a hierarchy with each level connected to the next and influencing each element. You can consider each level personally, or involve a team of people you are working with. Each level provides different information to clarify your understanding.

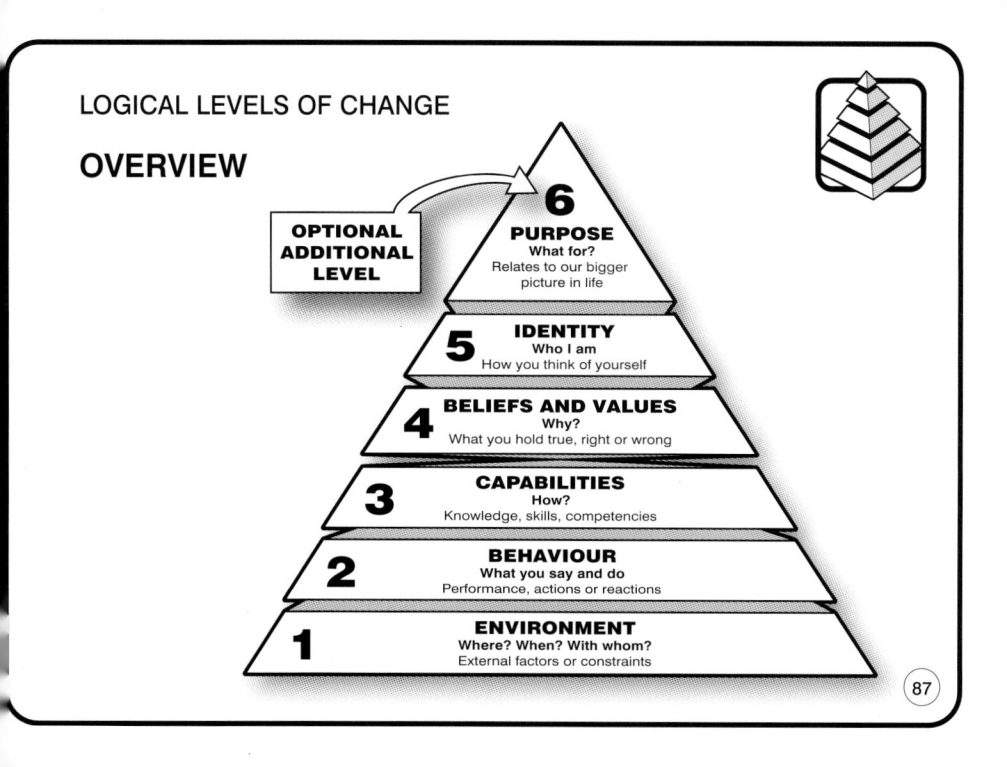

LOGICAL LEVELS OF CHANGE

OVERVIEW

OPTIONAL ADDITIONAL LEVEL

6 PURPOSE
What for?
Relates to our bigger picture in life

5 IDENTITY
Who I am
How you think of yourself

4 BELIEFS AND VALUES
Why?
What you hold true, right or wrong

3 CAPABILITIES
How?
Knowledge, skills, competencies

2 BEHAVIOUR
What you say and do
Performance, actions or reactions

1 ENVIRONMENT
Where? When? With whom?
External factors or constraints

LOGICAL LEVELS OF CHANGE
HOW THEY CAN HELP

Logical levels can help to:
- Clarify how you perceive a situation, eg your thoughts and ideas, what the real issues are
- Highlight at what level work needs to be done to achieve change or how you may need to intervene or interact
- Identify where a problem may come from, eg within an organisation or relationship, to help find a solution to move forward

Whilst learning and change can occur at different levels, change is usually easier in the context of the first level 'environment', eg by moving furniture. Change at a higher logical level usually impacts the lower levels. However, change at a lower level will not always affect change at a higher level.

Therefore, to solve a problem at one level, a change may be required at a different level first, eg you may want to change your behaviour but are struggling because the change may be linked to another logical level, which you need to address first.

LOGICAL LEVELS OF CHANGE

UNDERSTANDING THE LEVELS

1. **Environment** – external factors including where you are and the people you need around you, time of day (if you prefer working in the morning or evening), where you physically need to be, office layout, working space (open plan, private office), colour of a room.

2. **Behaviour** – the actions necessary to carry out a task, what you do and your specific actions, eg complete a project, write a report, commence a new task.

3. **Capabilities** – related to the knowledge, skills or talents you may have physically and mentally, and can repeat consistently, eg playing an instrument, being skilled in a particular sport, knowing how to use a computer package. New skills can be learned and, with a positive attitude and desire, capabilities can expand around you.

LOGICAL LEVELS OF CHANGE

UNDERSTANDING THE LEVELS

4. **Beliefs and values** – relates to a deeper, personal level linked to what you believe to be true and reinforces your motivation, eg do you believe the project will give you value, what factors are important to you, what value do you perceive in learning a new skill?

5. **Identity** – your sense of self, who you are, how you describe and express yourself.

6. **Purpose** – your mission in life or degree of 'passion', eg what you want to achieve, the company or personal mission, what contribution you want to make, your personal strengths.

LOGICAL LEVELS OF CHANGE

IDENTIFYING THE DIFFERENT LEVELS

The following sentence highlights five of the key levels. Where the person places emphasis on the word will often highlight which level they need to address to take action.

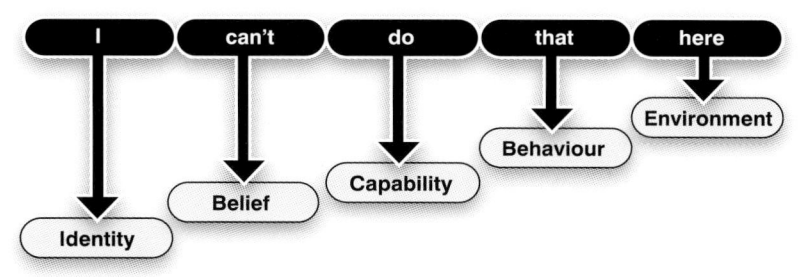

I	can't	do	that	here
Identity	Belief	Capability	Behaviour	Environment

To understand the different levels, it is important to listen clearly to ascertain where emphasis and intonation are placed. Further questions can then be asked related to the specific level, to find out what would help the individual make a positive change or move forward.

LOGICAL LEVELS OF CHANGE

IDENTIFYING THE DIFFERENT LEVELS

<u>I</u> can't do that here   Emphasis at IDENTITY level
Eg: **who** could do the task, or what could **you** do?

I **can't** do that here   Emphasis on BELIEF level
Eg: **why, what** factors are important to help you continue?

I can't **do** that here   Emphasis on CAPABILITY level
Eg: **how**, do you need additional skills or knowledge to proceed?

I can't do **that** here   Emphasis on BEHAVIOUR level
Eg: **what** actions can the person do? Does the task have a positive intention and link with your personal development?

I can't do that **here**   Emphasis on ENVIRONMENT
Eg: **where, when** or **with whom** could you take action?
Where do you need to work? What time of the day will be best?
Where do you need to be to do the task?

LOGICAL LEVELS OF CHANGE

PRACTICAL APPLICATIONS

'Significant problems cannot be solved at the same level of thinking with which we created them.'
Albert Einstein

Logical levels can be used in a variety of business situations to help create change. Ask questions to ascertain at which logical level the situation or problem has occurred and then phrase questions related to that specific level to find a way forward.

- **Project management:** eg task prioritisation and role responsibility. At the level of 'identity' you may ascertain that **you** cannot do the task, who else in the team you think can, or which task **you** can do

- **Providing a structure** to address different business issues – covering each logical level, eg where it will take place (environment), what needs to be done (behaviour), how to complete a task (capability), why it is important (belief), who is responsible (identity)

- **Problem-solving**: eg understand at which level a problem is based and where and how an intervention is required. This can help change the way of thinking and provide a route to move forward, eg by changing where you are working (environment) or whether you believe it is worthwhile (belief)

LOGICAL LEVELS OF CHANGE
PRACTICAL APPLICATIONS

- **Improving relationships and teamwork:** eg by asking questions related to each level – Who needs help? What has been said? What needs to be done to improve rapport?
- **Addressing business change:** eg highlighting and prioritising areas for change, who will be involved (identity), what skills will be needed (capability), where the change will occur (environment), why it is important (beliefs), and communicating the bigger picture (purpose)
- **Gathering information or preparing presentations:** creating a comprehensive approach, ensuring each logical level is covered in order to provide structure and detail
- **Monitoring and assessing situations:** eg at what level is the real issue and what do you need to change at that level to improve the situation? For example, a manager is frustrated with a team member for not producing the expected results. The manager relates to the person at an identity level (*'Why didn't YOU do that?'*) instead of ascertaining WHAT the individual needs in order to get the results (*'What will enable you to do this task?'*)

Your personal resources

YOUR PERSONAL RESOURCES

ACCESSING YOUR SKILLS

Your personal resources are the skills you have inside you which are developed during your many life experiences. In accessing your skills you may ask friends and colleagues to help, and you may learn new skills by training in new areas.

Beliefs often used in NLP:

'We have all the resources we need, we just need to learn how to access them to achieve excellence.'
(Relates to our state of mind.)

'You cannot teach a man anything. You can only help him discover it within himself.'
Galileo

'If you want one year of prosperity, grow seeds. If you want 10 years of prosperity, grow trees. If you want 100 years of prosperity, grow people.'
Chinese proverb

YOUR PERSONAL RESOURCES

NINE RULES FOR BEING HUMAN

The 'nine rules' highlight some positive resources linked to your beliefs. Consider which ones you relate to:

1. You get a body whether you like it or not – it's yours, use it well
2. You learn lessons in life whether you like it or not
3. There are no mistakes, only lessons – failed experiments are part of the process
4. Lessons are repeated until they are learned in various forms
5. Learning lessons doesn't end – there are always more lessons to learn
6. Over *there* is no better than *here*, but it will always look better than *here*!
7. Other people are mirrors of you – you may love or hate them depending on how you feel about yourself. What are they mirroring in you?
8. You have all the tools necessary – what you do is your decision
9. The answers are inside you – just look, listen and trust

Adapted from *'If Love is a Game, These are the Rules'* by Cherie Carter-Scott.

YOUR PERSONAL RESOURCES

CREATING A RESOURCE BANK

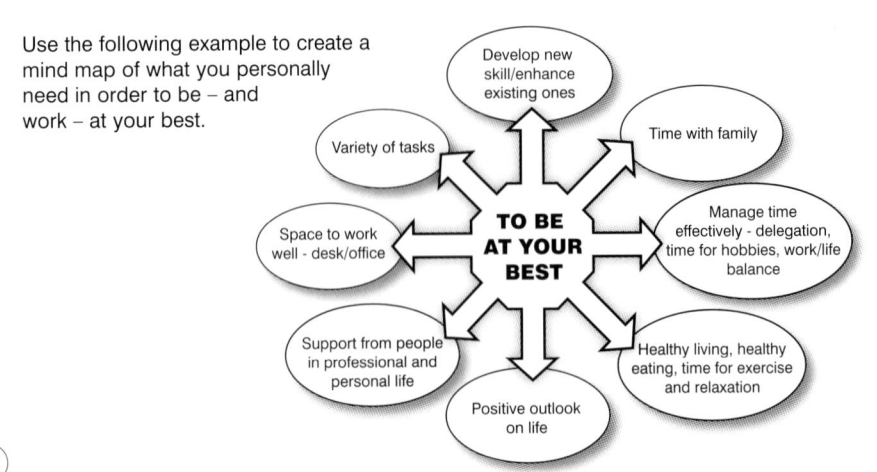

Use the following example to create a mind map of what you personally need in order to be – and work – at your best.

Mind map branching from **TO BE AT YOUR BEST**:

- Develop new skill/enhance existing ones
- Variety of tasks
- Time with family
- Space to work well - desk/office
- Manage time effectively - delegation, time for hobbies, work/life balance
- Support from people in professional and personal life
- Healthy living, healthy eating, time for exercise and relaxation
- Positive outlook on life

YOUR PERSONAL RESOURCES

CIRCLE OF EXCELLENCE

The 'Circle of Excellence' is a powerful way of mentally rehearsing a future situation. It helps you to access resources you will need and to imagine stepping into the experience before it occurs. The steps are:

1. Create a circle on the floor using a hoop or piece of string or by simply visualizing it.

2. Think of a future, challenging situation – eg a presentation, interview or difficult meeting. Taking the presentation as an example, consider the audience, key messages, preferred style, desired outcome, time allowed, etc.

3. Decide what skills/resources you'll need. For a presentation they will be confidence, clarity, familiarity with A/V equipment, ability to think freely to answer questions, good time management, relaxed body posture, controlled breathing/nerves, knowledge of topic, ability to create rapport, etc.

YOUR PERSONAL RESOURCES
CIRCLE OF EXCELLENCE

4. Recall past experiences (eg a previous successful presentation) when you have had those resources that you will need for the new challenge.

5. Step into the circle and relive that past experience. Involve all the senses: visualize yourself, experience the feelings and listen to the sounds. Use an anchoring technique – eg touch your arm or connect your thumb and middle finger – as you think of the positive resource.

6. Repeat step 5 for each of the resources you need (this strengthens the resources). Notice how differently you feel.

YOUR PERSONAL RESOURCES

CIRCLE OF EXCELLENCE

7. See yourself at the event (future pacing) with all the skills/resources available to you, as if they were flowing into your body, and see the event occurring in your mind's eye.

8. Step out of the circle.

9. Test how you feel by thinking about the challenging event, to see if there are any further resources required. Returning to the example presentation, feel, hear and see yourself successfully making the presentation as if it is taking place *now*. Do this with as much detail as possible, noting what you're wearing, what people are saying, how you're feeling, etc.

Future pace: think of other challenges you may have to face in the future. If further presentations, see yourself successfully delivering them with the resources you have already identified.

YOUR PERSONAL RESOURCES

CIRCLE OF EXCELLENCE

EXAMPLES OF POSITIVE RESOURCES

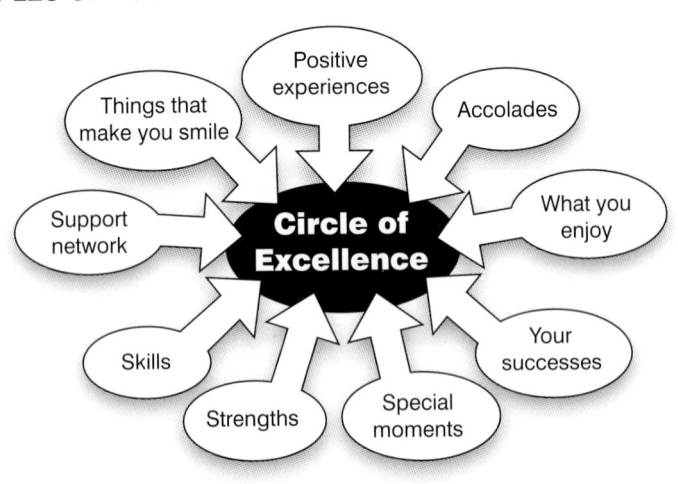

- Positive experiences
- Things that make you smile
- Accolades
- Support network
- What you enjoy
- Skills
- Your successes
- Strengths
- Special moments

Circle of Excellence

YOUR PERSONAL RESOURCES

ANCHORS

An anchor is a stimulus which reminds you of events and can change your state positively or negatively. The stimulus can involve all the senses (eg something you see, hear, feel, taste or smell) and can be internal or external.

An *internal* anchor is generated in your mind, eg as you remember a visual image which evokes certain feelings. An *external* anchor can be triggered when, for example, you hear a piece of music which reminds you of a lovely holiday or experience.

When to use them

When you feel unhappy or in a negative frame of mind, you can create a more resourceful state by triggering positive anchors in your mind and body. You can also create positive anchors for a future situation which is causing you concern (see 'future pacing', page 107).

YOUR PERSONAL RESOURCES

ANCHORS TO TRIGGER POSITIVE FEELINGS

EXAMPLES

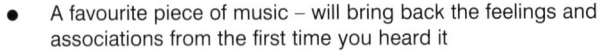

- A favourite piece of music – will bring back the feelings and associations from the first time you heard it
- An aroma – fresh coffee, perfume, etc
- An outdoor scene – eg a picture of a peaceful garden or view can bring an instant feeling of relaxation
- A memory of something you did really well when you were at your best – eg winning an award or competition
- A special holiday destination where you felt very relaxed
- A building or room in which you felt comfortable and in harmony with your environment
- A favourite item of clothing – wearing it will give you a sense of confidence

YOUR PERSONAL RESOURCES

CREATING POSITIVE ANCHORS

- Identify how you want to feel, physically, mentally or emotionally in order to achieve the desired resourceful state
- Create a detailed list or picture of your most resourceful states as you recall situations when you were feeling at your best. Try the following anchors – **kinaesthetic**: placing your thumb and middle finger together, placing your hand on your abdomen, placing hands together, standing tall or breathing deeply; **auditory**: using a phrase to give you confidence or playing a piece of music to create the right atmosphere; **visual**: anchor with a colour or scene
- Repeat the exercise several times to connect your chosen movement, phrase or picture with the positive state you want to anchor. Practise anchoring many good experiences to make the anchors more powerful
- Use all the senses to create your anchors: **Visual** – a positive image, a colour, a scene; **Auditory** – a positive saying, piece of music, phrase; **Kinaesthetic** – a feeling of confidence; **Olfactory** – an aroma that you associate with success or that gives you confidence; **Gustatory** – a taste that boosts your spirits.

YOUR PERSONAL RESOURCES

CREATING POSITIVE ANCHORS
SPORTING EXAMPLES

- You may recall the anchor practised by Jonny Wilkinson during the Rugby World Cup in 2003. To get into his resourceful state to score a goal he placed his hands together in a particular way

- A young friend who is a golfer passed his driving test by first creating positive anchors linked to successful golf competitions. His anchors included a positive phrase, seeing a colour in his mind and deep breaths. They helped him achieve the resourceful state to be mentally alert and successful

YOUR PERSONAL RESOURCES

FUTURE PACING AND MENTAL REHEARSAL

Future pacing takes the anchors you have developed into future situations. You are able to see yourself successfully managing a situation with more confidence or completing a task positively.

The mental rehearsal allows your mind and body time to practise the skills, to support your success before the event actually occurs.

Using kinaesthetic anchors, or writing information down, also brings the messages into the body's muscles, making the technique more powerful.

> *'Knowledge is only rumor until we feel it in our muscles.'*
> **Ancient saying from the American Indians**

YOUR PERSONAL RESOURCES

THE SCORE MODEL

The SCORE model helps to resolve issues in relation to achieving goals and moving from a difficult or challenging situation. Each of the letters relates to an aspect of the model:

Symptoms What you notice and what you would like to change about the present problem or problem state

Causes The root of the problem, where it came from

Outcomes Your goal, what you want

Resources What is required to resolve the situation, eg skills, tools, beliefs

Effects What you will do differently in the future, the longer-term effect of reaching the outcome

Ref: Judith DeLozier and Robert Dilts

YOUR PERSONAL RESOURCES

HOW TO 'WALK THE SCORE'

Symptoms
Problem state

Outcomes
What you want

Effects
Longer-term effect of achieving outcome

Causes
Where the problem comes from

Resources
What is required

YOUR PERSONAL RESOURCES

HOW TO 'WALK THE SCORE'

EXAMPLE

You have a project running late and need to turn it around. On separate pieces of paper write down the five words shown below in capital letters and place them on the floor. In the order shown, step on to each word and consider the questions related to your goal:

1. Identify the OUTCOME first – what you want to achieve (eg to ensure the project is successfully completed in an agreed time-frame).

2. Define the desired EFFECT – what you want in the longer-term (eg set up a process to ensure that projects are completed on time in future).

3. Consider the SYMPTOM – what's stopping completion of the task. Identify any barriers interfering with your goal (eg deadlines missed, customer complaints).

4. Define the CAUSE (eg the person running the project does not have the skills/experience required).

5. Step back from the words on the paper and consider your findings from the above. This helps identify the appropriate action required.

6. Identify the RESOURCES you need to achieve the desired outcome (eg training, additional personnel, a dedicated project manager).

COMPELLING ACTIONS

COMPELLING ACTIONS

IDENTIFYING BARRIERS TO ACTIONS BASED ON YOUR BELIEFS

Barriers can affect you throughout your life and delay you in achieving your goals and dreams. Barriers may be related to your capabilities, clarity, possibilities or the tasks involved. The following statements can help highlight any areas that may be delaying you making a start and moving forward. They will help you ascertain what you need to address in order to help you achieve your goal.

1.	My goal is desirable and worthwhile.	1 2 3 4 5
2.	It is possible to achieve my goal.	1 2 3 4 5
3.	What I have to do to achieve my goal is clear, appropriate and ecological. (In this context ecological means that the outcome fits in with your lifestyle.)	1 2 3 4 5
4.	I have the capabilities necessary to achieve my goal.	1 2 3 4 5
5.	I deserve to achieve my goal.	1 2 3 4 5

(See exercise on next page)

COMPELLING ACTIONS

IDENTIFYING BARRIERS TO ACTIONS BASED ON YOUR BELIEFS

Exercise

- Choose a goal for this exercise and write it down so it is clear in your mind
- Insert your goal into the five statements on the previous page and then say each statement aloud
- For each statement, rate your degree of belief in your goal, with 1 being the lowest and 5 the highest degree of belief. The lowest scores will highlight areas you need to work on initially, whilst the higher scores show you areas you feel more positive about
- Be aware of how you feel and what thoughts go through your mind as you score each statement. These thoughts may provide some useful messages during this exercise
- Ask yourself what else you need to help address the areas highlighted, eg if you score a low number for statement 4 in relation to 'capabilities', you will need to consider what specifically you need to do to have the capabilities to achieve your goal
- Once you have assessed your degree of confidence in these areas of belief, consider:
  - Are there other resources you need?
  - Do you need other people to help you in any way?

Adapted from Robert Dilts, Suzi Smith and Tim Hallbom

COMPELLING ACTIONS

THE TIME LINE PROCESS

The Time Line® process was designed by Tad James and is used for many aspects of personal development and problem-solving. A Time Line shows how an individual organises time. It can show pictorially where you see time and how you relate to time in your life. There is no right or wrong way as each person is different, and it is unique to each individual. Understanding how you relate to time is a key step in creating realistic future goals. You may relate to time in one of the following ways:

- Some people see themselves as 'being in the moment', more spontaneous, taking life as it comes, preferring not to plan or have deadlines – in NLP this is referred to as '**in time**'. Conversely, other people see events sequentially, taking more time to plan and make decisions – referred to as '**through time**'.

- Pictorial representation – you may also see time in different ways, eg some people think of the future by looking forward and of the past by looking back. Alternatively, you may look to the left when thinking about the past, or to the right when thinking about the future, or vice versa

COMPELLING ACTIONS

TIME LINE PROCESS FOR CREATING GOALS

The following process can be used to bring a goal into your Time Line. First, find a quiet area where you can relax without interruptions and then:

Step 1 – Create an achievable outcome

Step 2 – Clearly represent your goal

Step 3 – Ascertain your own Time Line

Step 4 – Use the Time Line with your goal

COMPELLING ACTIONS

TIME LINE PROCESS FOR CREATING GOALS

Step 1 – Create an achievable outcome, your goal
State exactly what your goal is and the intention behind it. This statement needs to be in the present tense, as if you are actually achieving it, and stated positively.

Step 2 – Clearly represent your goal
Involve all the senses to help bring your goal 'alive', so you can imagine yourself actually achieving your desired outcome. Make your representation as colourful and realistic as possible, with all the appropriate sounds and feelings going through your body:

- What will it look like?
- What will you hear or what will people be saying?
- What will you feel?

Some people find it useful to take several deep breaths at this stage to bring energy to their goal. This is a personal choice. However, remembering to breathe and stay relaxed throughout will understandably be as important!

COMPELLING ACTIONS

TIME LINE PROCESS FOR CREATING GOALS

Step 3 – Ascertain your own Time Line
To help ascertain your own Time Line, answer the two questions bulleted below. Note where you move your eyes or where you point as you answer. You may want someone to ask you the questions so they can observe your initial reactions and unconscious movement:

- If you think of the *past*, where do you look or where would you point?

- If you think of the *future*, where do you look or where would you point?

There is no right or wrong answer, what is important is where you elicit time. Some people may look to the left or point behind them when they think of the past, and some people instinctively look to the right or straight ahead when they think of the future.

When you have ascertained where you look, imagine a line going from the past to the future. This line will be used with the goal you are working on. Some people imagine the line like a piece of string or they may picture walking down a garden, along a favourite path or along a beach. Others just 'feel' their Time Line around them.

COMPELLING ACTIONS

TIME LINE PROCESS FOR CREATING GOALS

Step 4 – Use the Time Line with your goal
This step brings your goal into the Time Line via visualization. Imagine you are floating above yourself: float out into the future above your imaginary Time Line. Take with you the clear picture, sounds and feelings associated with your goal (defined in Step 2). As you reach the imaginary place and time where you want to achieve your goal, allow your goal to be inserted into the Time Line beneath you.

You may see in your mind's eye certain events change to help you achieve and support your goal, and you may be aware of people who will help you in the process. Whilst this is happening, you may also think of extra resources you need to help achieve your goal. Then float back in your imagination to now, knowing that your goal is firmly fixed on your Time Line.

This model helps bring your goal into the present tense and takes your body through a mental rehearsal of your goal actually happening, almost bringing it into your muscles and body. Start by using the process on the first goal that came into your mind whilst reading this section!

COMPELLING ACTIONS

THE TIME LINE PROCESS: SUMMARY

To realize your goals and visualize your successful outcome:

ESTABLISH A TIME LINE FROM PAST TO FUTURE

1. See yourself now on the Time Line.
2. Go back five years – where were you, what were your beliefs, and what influence does that have on you now?
3. Project yourself into the future, five years from now.
4. What do you want to continue, want more of: physically, spiritually, emotionally, socially?
5. Consider your lifestyle, habits, recreation, career, health.
6. Think of 10 attributes you would like to have.
7. Move five years on into the future and into your ideal self. Fully experience your future self.
8. Look back at your present self – what steps do you need to take?
9. Return to the present to view the ideal future self.

COMPELLING ACTIONS

REALIZING AND VISUALIZING YOUR GOALS

Using your senses and your imagination can have a powerful effect on making your goals realistic and compelling. The more details you can add, as if it is happening now, the more powerful and effective the technique is in turning your goals into reality. Be clear what you want and what obstacles you may need to overcome. 'See' and 'experience' your outcome as if it exists already – then you will have created a compelling goal.

10 steps for goal-setting

1. Have goals for all areas of your life – business, professional, career, family, health, finances, etc.
2. Include both short- and long-term goals.
3. Write down your goals so they become more than just a wish. There is growing evidence to show that writing down your goals makes you 50% more likely to achieve them.
4. State your goals in the positive:
   - What do you want?
   - What will that do for you?

COMPELLING ACTIONS

REALIZING AND VISUALIZING YOUR GOALS

5. Visualize yourself achieving your goals, visualize your success by vividly imagining and seeing yourself accomplishing your goals.
6. Define specifically what the outcome will be, involving all the senses:
    - How will you *know* that you have achieved it?
    - What will you be *seeing* when you have achieved it?
    - What will you be *hearing* when you have achieved it?
    - What will you be *feeling* when you have achieved it?
    - What will *someone else see you doing* when you've achieved it?
    - What will you *hear yourself saying* when you've achieved it?
7. Ensure you have the resources you need.
8. When do you want to achieve your goals? Have a clearly defined time frame.
9. Establish the first step you need to take, and then decide on the next steps.
10. When are you going to start? Confirm a date or time when you will start.

COMPELLING ACTIONS

THE GEO GOAL-SETTING MODEL

The GEO model helps you define key elements of your goal. It covers the essential aspects of your goal, the evidence and the desired outcome. It provides a feedback element to ensure you have clear goals, a way of knowing when you are close to achieving them, and the steps you need to take in order to reach them.

GOAL: Where you are now (present state), where you want to be (desired state) and the resources you need to help you achieve your goal.

PRESENT STATE ✚ RESOURCES* ≡ DESIRED STATE

*(including skills or training you may need)

EVIDENCE: Sensory-based, how you will know you have achieved your goal.

OUTCOME/OPERATION: Actions to achieve your goal.

COMPELLING ACTIONS

GOAL-SETTING USING THE GEO MODEL

Complete the following table to make a start now on your goals.

GOALS	**E**VIDENCE	**O**UTCOME OR OPERATION
Present state or problem – where are you? Desired state or outcome – where do you want to go?	How you know you've met your goals. What will it look like? What will it feel like? What will people say? How will others know? Is it win-win?	Actions to achieve the outcome and back-up plan. What contingencies will you need in place?
Your goals:	**Your evidence:**	**Your actions:**

Ref: Adapted from Robert Dilts

COMPELLING ACTIONS

WISE WORDS

> 'It's not what happens, it's what you do about it that makes the difference.'
> **Nelson Mandela made this statement in prison where he was preparing every day to be ready to lead.**

> 'We must become the change we want to see.'
> **Ghandi**

> 'Do not wait, the time will never be just right. Start, where you stand and work with whatever tools you may have at your command, and better tools will be found as you go along.'
> **Napoleon Hill**

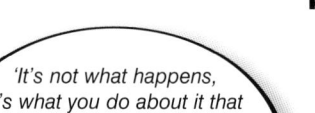

COMPELLING ACTIONS

CREATING MASTERY THROUGH LEARNING

There are four stages to learning a new skill such as NLP:

UNCONSCIOUS INCOMPETENCE   Learning a new skill for the first time, not knowing what you don't know.

CONSCIOUS INCOMPETENCE   Realizing what you don't know and what you still need to learn.

CONSCIOUS COMPETENCE   Building the new skill and capability, and feeling more familiar with them.

UNCONSCIOUS COMPETENCE   Expertly using the tools as if they were second nature, like driving a car.

Enjoy creating your own mastery with NLP!

FURTHER READING/RESOURCES

Anchor Point.
Articles and publications on NLP
www.nlpanchorpoint.com

International Teaching Seminars (ITS)
Run training courses in NLP, workshops and seminars
www.itsnlp.com
Tel: +44 (0)1268 777 125
(including Ian McDermott, Robert Dilts, Tim Hallbom – timh@nlpca.com, Suzi Smith – www.suzismith.net,)

John Seymour Associates
Run training courses in NLP
www.john-seymour-associates.co.uk
Tel: +44 (0) 845 658 0654

NLP University
Offer training and resources on NLP
www.nlpu.com (Robert Dilts, Judith DeLozier)

NLP Resources Catalogue
Available for download as pdf file from The Anglo American Book Company Ltd www.nlpbooks.com
Tel: +44 (0) 1267 211 880

Performance Partnership Ltd
Training courses in NLP
www.performancepartnership.com
Tel: +44 (0) 208 992 9523
(including David Shephard)

PPD Learning Ltd
Training courses in NLP
www.ppdlearning.co.uk
Tel: +44 (0) 807 7744 321 (including Judith Lowe, Joseph O'Connor, David Gordon, Judith DeLozier, Charles Faulkner, Christina Hall)

Robert Dilts
E-mail: rdilts@nlpu.com
Tel: 001 (831) 438 8571

Sue Spencer-Knight
Runs training courses in NLP for people in business
www.sueknight.co.uk
Tel: +44 (0) 1628 604 438

Time Line Therapy® Association Inc, 615 Piikoi Street, Suite 501 Honolulu, Hawaii 96814
Tel: 001 (808) 596 7765
E-mail: tlta@hypnosis.com
(including Tad James)

The Lazarus Consultancy
Jeremy Lazarus runs training courses in NLP and Time Line Therapy®, see www.thelazarus.com
Tel: + 44 (0) 20 8349 2929

University Press
Provides seminars, books and materials relating to NLP.
www.nlpuniversitypress.com

Books
NLP for Dummies
Romilla Ready and Kate Burton, published by Wiley,
ISBN 0764570285

Molecules of Emotion
Dr C B Pert, published by Simon & Schuster, ISBN 0684819813

The Human Mind and How to Make the Most of it
Professor Robert Winston, published by Bantam Press, ISBN 0593 052102

Your Mind at Work
Israel, Whitten and Shaffran, published by Kogan Page, ISBN 0749430591

About the Author

Gillian Burn, MSc in Exercise and Health

Gillian is Director of Health Circles Ltd, providing training and consultancy services focusing on improving health and quality of life for individuals and companies nationwide. Her background is in the health field, spanning over 25 years and covering nursing, midwifery and health visiting. Gillian is a master practitioner in Neuro-Linguistic Programming (NLP) and Time Line Therapy® which she uses in workshops with companies and coaching for individuals. Her workshops focus on training people to use their minds and bodies to increase energy and resilience. This includes nutrition and exercise advice, understanding the mind and body connection, creating balance in our lives, and techniques to increase creativity and effectiveness.

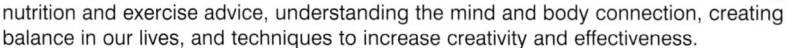

She is a licensed instructor with Tony Buzan for training in Mind Mapping® techniques and has trained in Mind Mapping, speed reading and memory techniques, and also runs training courses in these areas. In addition, Gillian is a trainer in Body Control Pilates Exercise. Gillian aims to practise what she preaches! She rows on the River Thames and enjoys swimming, walking, yoga and pilates.

Contact

Giliian can be contacted at: +44 (0) 1628 666 069 and via www.healthcircles.co.uk

ORDER FORM

Your details

Name _____

Position _____

Company _____

Address _____

_____

_____

Telephone _____

Fax _____

E-mail _____

VAT No. (EC companies) _____

Your Order Ref _____

Please send me: No. copies

The <u>NLP</u> Pocketbook ☐

The _____ Pocketbook ☐

The _____ Pocketbook ☐

The _____ Pocketbook ☐

The _____ Pocketbook ☐

Order by Post
MANAGEMENT POCKETBOOKS LTD
LAUREL HOUSE, STATION APPROACH,
ALRESFORD, HAMPSHIRE SO24 9JH UK
Order by Phone, Fax or Internet
Telephone: +44 (0)1962 735573
Facsimile: +44 (0)1962 733637
E-mail: sales@pocketbook.co.uk
Web: www.pocketbook.co.uk

MANAGEMENT POCKETBOOKS